1 MONTH OF
FREE
READING

at

www.ForgottenBooks.com

By purchasing this book you are eligible for one month membership to ForgottenBooks.com, giving you unlimited access to our entire collection of over 1,000,000 titles via our web site and mobile apps.

To claim your free month visit:
www.forgottenbooks.com/free908368

ISBN 978-0-266-91020-6
PIBN 10908368

This book is a reproduction of an important historical work. Forgotten Books uses
state-of-the-art technology to digitally reconstruct the work, preserving the original format
whilst repairing imperfections present in the aged copy. In rare cases, an imperfection in
the original, such as a blemish or missing page, may be replicated in our edition. We do,
however, repair the vast majority of imperfections successfully; any imperfections that
remain are intentionally left to preserve the state of such historical works.

Harvesting Pyrethrum

By A. F. Sievers, *senior biochemist,* and M. S. Lowman, *assistant biochemist, Division of Drug and Related Plants, Bureau of Plant Industry,* and W. M. Hurst, *agricultural engineer, Division of Farm Mechanical Equipment, Bureau of Agricultural Chemistry and Engineering* [1]

CONTENTS

INTRODUCTION

The commercial insecticide pyrethrum consists of the dried flowers of several species of *Chrysanthemum,* the most important source being *C. cinerariaefolium* (Trev.) Bocc., which has long been cultivated in southeastern Europe and Japan. The possibilities of this crop in the United States have been the subject of study by various individuals and agencies, and numerous trial plantings in various localities have shown that the crop is adapted to many sections and that flowers can be produced in this country which are equal or superior to those obtained from abroad. These studies have also demonstrated that the cost of production is considerable and that the cost of picking the flowers by the methods used in foreign countries would be prohibitive in the United States because of the hand labor required. It is obvious, therefore, that if this country is to produce its own requirements of pyrethrum a practical method of mechanical harvesting must be found that will reduce the cost sufficiently to permit reasonable net returns to the grower.

In 1934 a cooperative investigation of the mechanical harvesting of pyrethrum was begun by the Division of Drug and Related Plants,

[1] Credit is due George R. Stafford, assistant farm mechanic, Bureau of Agricultural Chemistry and Engineering, for assistance in constructing and operating the experimental machines.

Bureau of Plant Industry, and the Division of Mechanical Equipment, Bureau of Agricultural Engineering. The principal objective was to design and construct a machine that would remove the flowers from the pyrethrum plants and deliver them in a condition that permits their use in the several insecticide preparations in which pyrethrum is the principal component. It is believed that the machine herein described, although not as efficient as desired under all conditions, demonstrates the principle of such a machine and suggests the lines on which a successful harvester may be built.

The field trials of the several machines built and tested were made on pyrethrum plots at the Arlington Experiment Farm, Arlington, Va., the United States Plant Introduction Station, Glenn Dale, Md., and the United States Umatilla Field Station, Hermiston, Oreg., of the Bureau of Plant Industry; at the Arthurdale Community, Reedsville, W. Va., in cooperation with the West Virginia Agricultural Experiment Station, and in commercial fields at Belleville, Pa., and several localities in Lancaster County, Pa.

IMPORTANCE OF PYRETHRUM AS AN INSECTICIDE

Pyrethrum is one of the oldest and best known plant insecticides. In powdered form it has for years been successfully used for controlling many household insects, being particularly effective against flies. The fact that it is harmless to man and animal has made it especially desirable for household use. In more recent years its range of usefulness was greatly increased through the introduction of extracts of the flowers, which contain the two active principles, pyrethrins I and II, on which the insecticidal properties of the flowers depend. These extracts, in suitable form, have come into wide use as household sprays and for control of insects in greenhouse and garden crops, either alone or in combination with other plant insecticides, particularly rotenone.

With such extensive use, the world's requirement of pyrethrum is naturally considerable, and its production is an agricultural industry of importance in a number of countries. The amount of pyrethrum used in the United States from 1923 to 1938 is indicated by the quantities imported, as given in table 1.

TABLE 1.—*Imports of pyrethrum flowers to the United States in the period 1923–1938, inclusive, and their declared values*

Year	Quantity	Value		Year	Quantity	Value	
		Total	Per pound			Total	Per pound
	Pounds	*Dollars*	*Cents*		*Pounds*	*Dollars*	*Cents*
1923	2,973,863	1,397,910	47.0	1931	4,521,143	522,103	11.5
1924	3,945,101	1,603,764	40.7	1932	12,110,736	1,309,092	10.8
1925	6,435,405	1,236,692	19.2	1933	10,434,559	1,523,749	14.6
1926	9,852,850	1,219,365	12.4	1934	10,590,771	2,059,492	19.4
1927	8,993,109	1,220,107	13.6	1935	15,572,058	2,041,993	13.1
1928	13,689,009	3,692,126	27.0	1936	11,756,979	943,271	8.0
1929	9,013,077	2,060,884	22.9	1937	20,091,596	2,204,451	11.0
1930	8,536,426	1,333,016	15.6	1938	14,537,417	2,490,870	17.1

WORLD SOURCES OF PYRETHRUM

Prior to the World War pyrethrum was obtained mainly from a number of provinces on the eastern Adriatic coast in what is now Yugoslavia. However, small plantings in Japan had shown earlier than that, that the crop was well adapted to certain sections of that country, and by 1910 the production there was becoming important. Thereafter the crop was rapidly extended in that country and for many years it was the chief source of the world's supply of pyrethrum. In recent years Kenya, Africa, has become an important source, and Brazil also is furnishing substantial quantities.

ATTEMPTS TO GROW PYRETHRUM COMMERCIALLY IN THE UNITED STATES

Pyrethrum was first grown in the United States in central California many years ago by a manufacturer of insect powder. Information concerning this early introduction of the crop is meager and available reports regarding it are conflicting. It is known, however, that production costs were excessive and that the most important item of cost was the hand-picking of the flowers. When the flowers became available from foreign sources at more moderate cost the crop was abandoned. Since then the only attempts to grow pyrethrum commercially were made in central and eastern Pennsylvania several years ago. The acreage was not large and interest in the crop could not be sustained because the cost of production was too high, primarily because too much labor was required in harvesting. Moreover, the harvesting had to be done at a time when other crops required much attention.

INVESTIGATIONS OF PYRETHRUM AS A DOMESTIC CROP

The possibilities of pyrethrum as a crop in the United States have been under investigation for some years by various individuals and agencies. In some States, particularly Colorado, Oregon, and Tennessee, the experiment stations have studied the crop. In many of the Eastern and Southern States its cultural requirements and adaptiveness were investigated by the experiment stations, through cooperation with R. E. Culbertson, working under a fellowship of the Crop Protection Institute. The Bureau of Plant Industry of the United States Department of Agriculture, also through the collaboration of experiment stations and other agencies, has likewise determined the agronomic requirements of the crop in widely scattered regions.

To a large extent these investigations have been concerned with the growing of the plant, the relation of soil, climate, and other factors to the yield of flowers and their insecticidal value, and with the development of better and more toxic strains. The information thus developed is of primary importance, but a demonstration of the adaptiveness of the crop to a region is not sufficient to warrant its recommendation to growers. Elimination of excessive hand labor in harvesting the flowers must be accomplished before pyrethrum growing in the United States on a large scale becomes possible even if all other considerations involved are favorable.

CHARACTERISTICS OF THE PLANT AND THEIR RELATION TO HARVESTING METHODS

Pyrethrum is a perennial plant grown from seed, but it may also be propagated by crown division. The seedlings are usually grown in a seedbed and, when 4 or 5 inches high, are transplanted to the field, being set 12 to 18 inches apart in rows from 2 to 3 feet apart. If set out in late spring the plants will develop an extensive system of fibrous roots and acquire a crown diameter of 6 to 12 inches under good conditions. They will not bloom the first year. A good crop of flowers is produced the second year and for several years thereafter if the proper cultural practices are followed.

The pyrethrum plant blooms during the period from early May to the middle of July. In the South and in the warm, dry regions of the Southwest and West the plants are in full bloom by the middle of May; in the central latitudes from late in May to the middle of June; and at high elevations as late as the latter part of July. In practically all regions, however, the harvest period comes at a time when various other crops require attention. Moreover, the harvesting must be accomplished during a relatively short time, because the flowers rapidly reach and pass the preferred stage for picking. These conditions and the slowness of the methods employed have made the harvesting of the flowers at the right time a serious problem to the few growers who planted small acreages of the crop in this country.

The growth characteristics of the pyrethrum plant and the nature of its flowers are shown in figure 1. The flower stems radiate from the crown, the flowers forming a dome at the top. The stems range in height from 15 to 40 inches and usually grow fairly upright but at times lean considerably or even lodge on the ground (fig. 1, B). This lodging is sometimes due to soil conditions that cause too rank growth or weak stems, but there are also certain strains or types of the plant that possess such growth habits. Such conditions are undesirable, because they make the harvesting of the flowers more difficult, regardless of the method used. No mechanical device, however efficient in removing the flowers from upright plants, can be expected to work satisfactorily when the plants are badly lodged and tangled. It is important, therefore, that plants of undesirable growth habits be eliminated by careful selection and that the soil be such that sturdy, upright growth is obtained.

The flower consists of a central disk of numerous small vertical tubular, yellow florets with an outer ring of ray florets, which have a white corolla. After the flower bud opens and the ray florets are fully expanded the small disk florets open gradually, beginning around the edge of the disk and progressing toward the center. The most desirable stage for picking the flowers is when one-half to three-fourths of the disk florets have opened. In the past the opinion prevailed

FIGURE 1.—Pyrethrum plants showing: *A*, Sturdy, upright growth, which greatly facilitates clean harvesting; *B*, rank growth and lodging, which make harvesting difficult.

that the insecticidal value of flowers in which about half of the disk florets are open is much greater than in the preceding or subsequent stages, but the difference in that respect in the several stages is at present not believed to be as important as was formerly assumed. When hand-picking is resorted to it is possible to go over the field several times, and thus pick only the flowers that are at the right stage. When any mechanical device or machine is used this of course cannot be done and consequently a crop so harvested is likely to consist of flowers of all stages, including some buds.

The flowers can usually be removed easily from the stems with a slight "plucking" motion, leaving little, if any, of the stem adhering to them. As they mature, especially in dry weather, the upper portion of the stem toughens and then more of the flowers come off with pieces of the stem attached to them (fig. 2). Under some conditions the stems pull off at the crown, in which case the harvested material includes considerable stems and leaves.

A practical machine for harvesting must meet a number of requirements. It must strip the flowers from normal upright stems without leaving more than a small percentage on the plants. The stripped flowers should not contain too much of the stems and leaves, although much of the "stemmy material"[2] can be removed with a fork or rake or some other suitable implement. Loose leaves and small pieces of stems cannot be separated readily from the fresh flowers but can be removed to a large extent with a fanning mill after the flowers are dry, as will be discussed later.

The machine must also be so designed that it is adaptable to the system of planting usually followed, especially with respect to the distance between the rows. The wheels of the machine must not run on the harvested rows because the plants will be damaged. Once a machine is available the spacing of the rows in plantings made thereafter should of course be such that the best performance may be secured. Pyrethrum prefers light, well-drained ground and is usually grown on sandy soil types on which difficulty in securing proper traction may be experienced. Moreover, under irrigation the plants are grown on ridges with irrigation furrows midway between the rows. These various conditions must be taken into consideration if the machine is to be practical under as many conditions as possible.

VARIOUS HARVESTING METHODS THAT ARE IN USE OR HAVE BEEN PROPOSED

The most primitive method of harvesting pyrethrum consists of picking the flowers by hand. It is a tedious procedure though neither exacting nor laborious and hence is frequently done by women and children. An efficient worker can pick 100 pounds of flowers a day, equivalent to approximately 25 pounds of dry flowers. In the United States, even in regions where the lowest wage scales prevail, the cost would be at least 4 or 5 cents a pound, which in some years would represent fully one-third of the market value of the

---

[2] The term "stemmy material" as used in this circular refers to the long stems with flowers and some leaves attached that are pulled from the plants by the mechanical harvester herein described.

FIGURE 2.—*A*, Pyrethrum flowers in the proper stage for harvesting. At this stage the stems are brittle and the flowers can be snapped off readily. *B*, Flowers from Belleville, Pa., 1937, showing the several stages of maturity when the field was harvested (see fig. 10). Most of these are overmature, their stems are tough, and it is difficult to pull them off.

flowers. Moreover, even moderate acreages in a community would require an excessive number of workers, because the harvesting must be accomplished in a short period.

A somewhat less tedious method involves the use of various hand-stripping devices. A box stripper, somewhat like that used for harvesting cranberries, is reasonably efficient when the plants are upright but useless if there is considerable lodging. The stripping edge of the box consists of a row of tenpenny nails, with heads removed, set firmly and close together and forming a sort of comb. A simple device of this sort being used by two persons working together is shown in figure 3. This method, though more laborious, is more rapid than hand-picking but still far too costly for domestic use. In still another method the flower stems are cut off with sickles just above the crown and then drawn through a comblike device attached to a table or rail, thereby stripping off the flowers.

FIGURE 3.—Harvesting pyrethrum flowers with a box stripper.

None of the above methods has received any serious consideration by investigators of the crop in this country. The last-mentioned method was employed in principle in Pennsylvania in recent years, but the stripping was accomplished with a power-driven machine. This consisted of a rapidly revolving cylinder provided with closely spaced spikes or teeth, and mounted in a simple box housing. Small bunches of the stems with flowers attached, cut with hand sickles, are held against the cylinder, revolving at about 700 r. p. m., which strips off the flowers and deposits them in the rear. The stems are discarded. Such a machine may be mounted with a small gasoline engine on a low-bodied truck or wagon and moved along in the field as the harvesting proceeds, or set up in a convenient building and the cut flowers hauled to it. It is necessary that the cut material be carefully handled, so that the flowers are all at one end of the bundle. It is reported that by this method seven persons can harvest about an acre a day. To pick the flowers from a similar area by hand, assuming a yield of 2,800 pounds of fresh flowers (700 pounds of dry flowers), would require the services of 28 persons working at the rate previously mentioned. This semimechanized method, therefore, reduces the cost of harvesting to about one-fourth that of hand-picking, but it is nevertheless too costly and much too slow to enable a grower to harvest a substantial acreage in the short time during which the flowers are at the right stage. It was found to be much too tedious to serve the purpose under the conditions prevailing in Pennsylvania (figs. 4 and 5).

Attempts have been made to utilize other available farm equipment for the purpose. Culbertson [3] experimented with a bluegrass stripper with some success. He found that the machine sometimes pulled plants out of the ground, but that it appeared to have possibilities if minor modifications were made. When the plants are grown on loose soils any device that depends for its action on the passing of

FIGURE 4.—Harvesting pyrethrum with sickles in Pennsylvania. The bunches of flowers are loaded on the small wagon in background and hauled to the barn where the flowers are removed from the stems with a stripping machine.

a rake or comb through the plant at one movement will very likely pull a considerable number of plants from the ground.

Other harvesting implements now in use on the farm have been tried, namely, the mower, reaper, and grain binder. These will not remove the flowers from the plants and their use depends on the feasibility of cutting the flowers with the stems, drying them in the field, and using the ground material as such as an agricultural dust, or separating the flowers when dry by some practical means. A mowing machine will cut off the flower stems cleanly if the plants are not lodged, but the cut material is raked up with difficulty because it is scattered over the ground and the crowns of the plants. This could be remedied by attaching a platform to the sickle bar and raking off the cut material in bunches into the space between

[3] Correspondence of R. E. Culbertson, formerly fellow on Pyrethrum Investigations, Crop Protection Institute.

256347°—41——2

the rows. A reaper would accomplish the same thing and probably be more efficient in this respect.

Experiments with a grain binder have shown that erect plants may be cut without difficulty and that the material can be bound with most of the flowers at one end of the bundles. However, there is usually enough tangling of the stems to make the removal of the flowers from the stems with the stripping machine referred to tedious and unsatisfactory. Field tests have demonstrated that such bundles, if loosely bound, will dry and cure in shocks even if moderate rain occurs (fig. 6). It was found that when thus cured and passed

FIGURE 5.—Harvesting pyrethrum in Pennsylvania. The flowers are cut with sickles (fig. 4) and then stripped from the stems with the machine mounted on the truck and powered by a small gasoline motor.

through a thresher with some adjustment of the air and screens, a good separation of the flowers and stems can be obtained. The flowers are thoroughly broken up and small proportions of broken stems and leaf material are included. In that form it should be acceptable for the manufacture of extracts to be used in field or greenhouse and as agricultural dusts but possibly not for commercial pyrethrum powder or for household sprays. It has been reported that when thus broken up the toxic principles present in the flowers undergo changes more rapidly than when the flower remains whole. If this is generally the case the threshed material would have to be extracted without delay, a requirement that cannot be complied with readily except through close cooperation between grower and manufacturer.

FIGURE 6.—Pyrethrum that has been cut with grain binder curing in shocks at Glenn Dale, Md.

EXPERIMENTAL HARVESTERS

A cotton stripper of the type sometimes used in northwest Texas was tried for harvesting pyrethrum in the 1935 season. The stripping unit on the machine consists of two rollers set substantially parallel at about 34° with the horizontal. The rollers are 3 inches in diameter and approximately 3 feet long. The front or lower ends are provided with lateral adjustment for varying the space between the rollers through which the plants pass as the machine is pulled along the row. The stripping bars on the rollers thus moving upward at each side of the plant strip the flowers from the stem. Originally the rollers were provided with teeth, but these were spaced too far apart for pyrethrum. They were removed and five angle-iron bars fastened to each of the rollers. These greatly improved the performance of the machine.

In the field tests all the material gathered by the machine on one or more rows selected for the test was separated by hand or with a fork into two portions. One, consisting mostly of clean flowers, included small quantities of leaf fragments and flowers with short stems attached. The other, already referred to as "stemmy material," consisted of longer stems with flowers and some leaves attached. The flowers left on the plant were picked by hand and those stripped from the plant that fell to the ground were picked up. By weighing these several portions the efficiency of the machine under the particular conditions could be determined.

The machine was very efficient when the crop was light and the plants were tall and upright, but under adverse conditions, that is, in a heavy, badly lodged crop, the performance was poor. Under such conditions the stripping rolls appeared to be too short and their speed too slow. The pick-up snouts for guiding the plants into the machine were also ineffective.

A new machine was constructed before the 1936 harvest in which longer rollers were used and provisions made for speed adjustments (fig. 7). Conveyors were provided for removing the stripped flowers from beneath the rollers to a container at the rear. Changes were also made in the pick-up snouts.

This machine was more effective in harvesting a heavy crop than the original, but further improvements were needed. The space between the revolving rollers and the edges of the troughs, in which the conveyors operated, permitted many flowers to fall through. The machine tended to push the plants forward and pass over some of the flowers that the snouts failed to guide between the rollers, indicating the need for an effective pick-up device. It required a side guard to lift up leaning or lodged plants from the adjoining row, so that the side wheel would not run over them. It was also obvious that a side hitch would be a great improvement, because it would eliminate the trampling and tangling of plants caused by one horse walking between two unharvested rows.

FIGURE 7.—Pyrethrum harvester used in the early experiments showing stripping rollers and conveyor belts for depositing stripped flowers in box at rear.

To remedy these several faults a third machine was built in which the stripping-rollers unit was mounted on a corn-binder frame and use was made of the binder bull wheel, side hitch, tongue truck, and pick-up chains (figs. 8 and 9). These and other changes greatly improved the harvester, as was demonstrated by the tests made in several localities in 1937 (table 2). Although this machine performed in a more satisfactory manner than previous models, there remained considerable work to be done in perfecting it (figs. 10, 11, and 12). Prior to the 1938 harvest season pick-up chains with longer lugs were installed as well as flexible pick-up guards (figs. 13 and 14). Means

FIGURE 8.—Front view of the machine built in 1937 in which part of a corn-binder frame and drive are utilized, showing how the plants move into the throat of the machine.

of changing quickly from staggered to opposed position of bars on the stripping rollers was provided for use in testing the machine for maximum efficiency. While the harvesting conditions at Glenn Dale, Md., where the machine was operated during the 1938 season, were favorable so far as concerns the condition of the plants, results of tests indicated nevertheless that the changes made tended to improve the performance of the machine and assured greater efficiency under more difficult conditions (table 2).

FIGURE 9.—View of throat of pyrethrum harvester in which the stripping rollers are built into a corn binder, showing the pick-up chains. The rough appearance of the ends of the rollers is due to a gummy material from the plants which is deposited on the rollers under some conditions.

FIGURE 10.—Field partly harvested with the machine at Belleville, Pa., 1937. The flowers were overmature (see fig. 2, *B*) and the stems were tough, due to dry weather. The machine was working here under very unfavorable conditions. (See table 2 for data.)

FIGURE 11.—Field at Reedsville (Arthurdale), W. Va., 1937, where the flower stems were abnormally short. Many of the flowers left on the plants slipped under the machine thus escaping the strippers. The fifth row from the right was cleaned up by hand.

FIGURE 12.—Harvesting a field of pyrethrum at Glenn Dale, Md., 1937.

TABLE 2.—*Machine performance as affected by various adjustments and speeds of the stripping bars and rollers*

Place, year, and No. of test	Rollers			Stripping bars		Crop harvested [1]		Field losses of flowers [1]			
	Spacing		Approximate speed	Number	Position	Flowers	Stemmy material [2]	On upright stems [3]	On down stems [4]	Stripped but on ground [5]	Total
	Top	Bottom									
	In.	In.	R.p.m.			Pct.	Pct.	Pct.	Pct.	Pct.	Pct.
Glenn Dale, Md., 1937:											
1	1⅝	1¾	600	5	Opposed	94.0	10.6	4.1	1.9		
2	1¾	2	800	5	___do___	91.4	4.1	5.4	3.2		
3	1¾	2	1,000	5	___do___	92.7	3.6	4.5	2.8		
Belleville, Pa., 1937:											
1	1⁹⁄₁₆	1⅞	600	5	___do___	78.2	15.7	5.1	4.2	12.5	21.8
2	1⁹⁄₁₆	1⅞	800	5	___do___	90.5	16.7	3.6	1.6	4.3	9.5
3	1⁹⁄₁₆	1⅞	1,000	5	___do___	85.8	15.2	2.3	2.9	9.0	14.2
4	1⁹⁄₁₆	1¹¹⁄₁₆	600	10	Staggered	89.4	8.4	2.4	5.2	3.0	10.6
Glenn Dale, Md., 1938:											
1	1½	1⅞	700	10	___do___	93.0	3.9	2.6	2.3	2.1	7.0
2	1⅝	2	700	10	Opposed	93.0	8.9	2.0	2.0	3.0	7.0
3	1⅝	1⅞	700	5	___do___	90.0	12.5	1.9	4.4	3.7	10.0

[1] All percentages calculated on the basis of fresh flowers weighed immediately after harvesting.
[2] The flowers included in this stemmy material are not included in the total percentage lost indicated in the last column. They constitute from 30 to 50 percent of this stemmy material, which makes this of some value for insecticide purposes when used by itself.
[3] Some of these passed between the rolls without being stripped off and others, although on upright stems, did not get into the throat of the machine.
[4] This includes flowers from all stems too prone on the ground from various causes to be lifted by the pick-up snouts.
[5] Most of these are lost by being thrown on the ground through the open front of the machine.

FIGURE 13.—Front view of machine as developed after several years' experimenting (1938). The special pick-up snouts and longer lugs on the pick-up chains have been added.

FIGURE 14.—Rear view of machine in use at Glenn Dale, Md., 1938, with tailboard removed showing conveyor belts, drives, and stripped flowers.

In the summer of 1939 the machine was used at the Umatilla field station of the Division of Irrigation Agriculture of the Bureau of Plant Industry at Hermiston, Oreg., where 1.7 acres of pyrethrum had been grown as a cooperative project for a number of years. This acreage is grown on sandy soil under irrigation and afforded an opportunity to test the machine under ground conditions not previously encountered. The irrigation water is applied through furrows that run midway between the rows, and the plants are growing on ridges from 4 to 6 inches above the irrigation furrows. Diffi-

FIGURE 15.—Pyrethrum field under irrigation at Hermiston, Oreg., showing performance of the harvester in 1939.

culty was experienced due to lack of sufficient traction in the rather loose soil when a team was used, but the machine performed well when pulled by a tractor. With substantial power thus obtained and a stripping roller speed of 1,000 r. p. m., the harvester was very efficient when the clearances between the rolls had been properly adjusted after a number of trials. The efficiency of the machine in this test is indicated by figure 15 and by the data in table 3.

TABLE 3.—*Data showing efficiency of pyrethrum harvester in tests on irrigated plot of pyrethrum at the Umatilla field station, Hermiston, Oreg., 1939*

Power	Rows 455 feet long	Material delivered by machine				Flowers left on plants [1]		Condition of harvested material
		Flowers and stems	Stemmy material		Stems [2]			
	Number	*Pounds*	*Pounds*	*Percent*	*Percent*	*Pounds*	*Percent*	
Horse	1	84.5	8.0	23.2	11.6	2	5.8	Considerable quantity of green leaves included.
Tractor	2	84.0	11.0	13.1	6.5	--------	--------	Flowers very clean.
	2	71.5	6.0	8.4	4.2	--------	--------	Do.
	2.5	76.5	4.5	5.9	2.9	--------	--------	Do.
	2	65.0	4.0	6.2	3.1	2	3.1	Do.
	2	55.0	4.0	7.3	3.6	--------	--------	Do.

[1] These were left on the plants because the flower stems slipped under the machine without going through the rolls and because stems were packed down on the ground by the tractor wheels. Uniform spacing of the rows and adjustment of the space between the rows should eliminate some of this loss.
[2] This column shows the percentage of stems in the material as delivered by the machine. These stems are a part of the stemmy material, a sample lot of which contained 46.2 percent of stems. The figures in this column are obtained on the basis of 50 percent of stems being present in the stemmy material.

DETAILS OF CONSTRUCTION AND EFFECTS OF VARIOUS MODIFICATIONS AND CONDITIONS ON PERFORMANCE AND EFFICIENCY

Although preliminary trials with the cotton-stripper-type machine indicated greater promise than any device yet tried, the speed of the rollers, number and position of the stripper bars, roller spacing, and adjustments influenced its performance. For these reasons development work was directed largely toward alterations and means of adjusting for maximum efficiency.

The salient features of the machine are diagrammatically illustrated in figures 16 and 17.

Referring to figure 16, self-aligning bearings on the rollers and universal joints make possible a wide range of lateral adjustment. The bearing supports at the top ends are slotted and the lower-end bearings are adjustably attached to the frame of the machine. A piece of channel iron welded to the frame provides a slide for an angle-iron support for each lower-end bearing. Because these bearing supports carry a part of the weight of the roller and the conveyors for the stripped flowers, and because of the resistance offered by the plant stems passing between the rollers, additional supports were necessary. A rod extending downward from a brace on the frame answered as an auxiliary support.

Considerable difficulty was experienced with the lower-end bearing support assembly, due to space requirements. It is necessary that the lower ends of the rollers extend almost to the ground, thus allowing very little room for the conveyor. The conveyor housing, if too close to the ground, cuts in on the side of the row and injures the plants when the machine is in operation. When the conveyor is installed to provide ample clearance, the trough for the conveyor is too shallow. In order to overcome these difficulties the lower

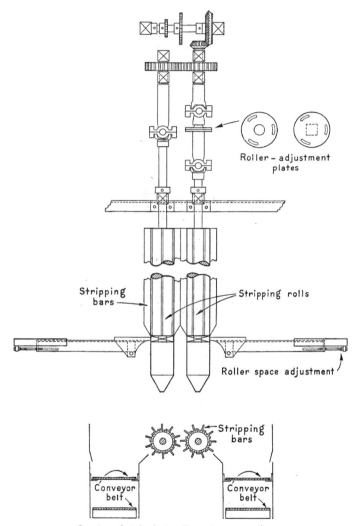

Roller - adjustment
plates

Stripping
bars

Stripping rolls

Roller space adjustment

Stripping
bars

Conveyor
belt

Conveyor
belt

Section of stripping rolls and conveyor boxes

FIGURE 16.—Salient parts of stripping mechanism on pyrethrum harvester.

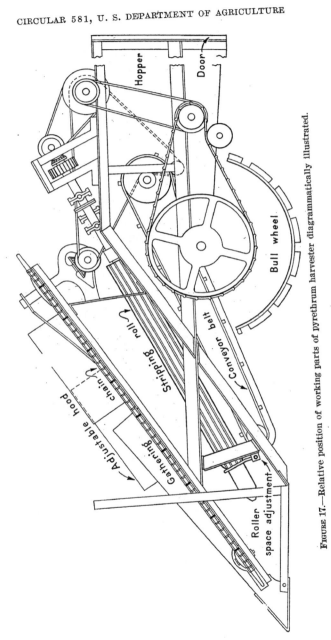

FIGURE 17.—Relative position of working parts of pyrethrum harvester diagrammatically illustrated.

end of the conveyor was set back of the bearing support and a piece of metal installed to guide back to the conveyor the flowers stripped by the lower ends of the rollers. However, the lower ends of the rollers in the experimental machine were not close enough to the ground for effective work in harvesting a short crop.

In designing a new machine, adjustment for the stripping rollers at the top would probably be unnecessary, especially if 4-feet or longer rollers are provided. With 3-inch rollers and ¾-inch stripping bars, the rollers might be set 4½ inches on centers at the top. Adjustment should be provided at the lower ends so that the rollers might be moved from possibly 4½ inches to a maximum of 6 inches on centers.

Stripping roller speed for most effective work seems to depend upon crop condition and the number of stripping bars used. A roller speed of 250 r. p. m. with 5 bars on each roller gave good results on a light crop under favorable field conditions. Under adverse conditions 10 bars and a roller speed of 600 r. p. m. might be required. In the tests recorded in table 2 a roller speed in excess of 600 r. p. m. did not seem to improve the effectiveness of the machine in removing the flowers from the plants, but at Hermiston, Oreg., a speed of 1,000 r. p. m. gave good results when the rollers were otherwise properly adjusted.

In a light crop and under favorable conditions opposed stripping bars gave as good results as when the bars were staggered, except that a higher percentage of stemmy material was delivered. When they are in opposed position the flowers are usually stripped from the plants with no stems or with long stems attached. With staggered bars there were fewer long stems, but more short ones. In a heavy or tough crop staggered bars gave best results, as is shown in table 2 for the Belleville, Pa., crop in 1937. The crop in this field was overripe and the plants were exceptionally tough, because of a dry season. In changing from 5 bars in opposed position to 10 bars staggered, the percentage of stemmy material was reduced from about 15 percent to approximately 8 percent.

A further improvement in performance can no doubt be obtained if the pick-up chains, stripping mechanism, and conveyor belts are powered by a gasoline motor mounted on the machine, which assures that these parts will operate at steady speed independent of the forward movement of the machine.

To obtain the best results with the machine it is essential that it move over the row at the proper speed, uniformly maintained. A team usually slows down when the machine encounters a heavy stand of plants with a corresponding reduction in the speed of the stripping rollers. This permits some of the flowers to slip through without being stripped off. A tractor with its sustained speed is therefore a much better source of power than a team for operating the machine.

Other factors that affect the efficiency of the machine require consideration. It is necessary that the rows be reasonably straight and evenly spaced, because it is essential that the plants enter squarely into the throat of the machine and this is impossible if the planting has been carelessly done. The contour and condition of the land are also factors affecting performance. The machine works better on level ground than on steep slopes and much better on smooth, firm ground than on loose or stony ground, which makes it more difficult for the driver to hold the machine directly over the row. If the flower stems are lodged too close to the ground the pick-up snouts will not get under them and bring them into the throat of the machine, but unless the plants have lodged badly through heavy rain and wind not many flowers will be lost that way. The tests at Reedsville, W. Va., demonstrated that when plants are much less than 18 inches high many of the flower stems will slip under the machine without going between the stripping rollers even when upright, and under some ground conditions this will happen when the plants are somewhat taller. Abnormally short plants will not be encountered frequently but may result when unusual drought occurs during the time when the flowers are developing. Very high ridges or deep furrows on irrigated land may at times cause trouble, unless the machine is especially designed to be used under such conditions.

A machine like the one described, if constructed of good materials, should give service comparable to that of other harvesting implements in general use. Because pyrethrum is grown in rows like corn and because the machine moves at a ground speed about that of a corn binder, it is estimated that the acreage that can be harvested in a day would compare somewhat with the acreage of corn harvested by a modern corn binder. The distance between the rows is, of course, a factor and allowance must be made for the stops required to remove the flowers from the hopper. With due consideration to these factors it is believed that under reasonably favorable conditions it should be possible to harvest about 4 acres a day.

Although one person can handle the machine alone it is advisable that the driver have a helper who will remove the flowers and assist in other ways that will tend to reduce the number and length of the stops. This is true whether a team or tractor is used. On that basis, therefore, the harvesting cost with this machine, so far as outlay for labor is concerned, may be compared roughly with that of the semimechanized method previously described. In that case seven persons are required to harvest 1 acre a day, whereas with this machine two persons can harvest about 4 acres. These estimates do not take into consideration the labor required to remove the flowers to the drying shed and for such handling as is necessary thereafter.

The efficiency of the machine as measured by the completeness of removal of the flowers from the plants is indicated by the data in tables 2 and 3. At Glenn Dale, Md., a maximum efficiency of 93 percent was obtained with the machine in 1938, but it should be pointed out that although the plants were in good condition the stony ground was an unfavorable factor. Moreover, many plants had died in this field, leaving open places in the rows. This always reduces the efficiency of the machine, because the flower stems of the plant entering the machine, if there is not another plant alongside of it, will push forward and slide under the machine.

Mention has been made of the difficulty encountered at Hermiston, Oreg., where the loose soil prevented sufficient traction when a team was used. Under such conditions the machine removed 94.2 percent of the flowers, but the harvested material included 23.2 percent of stemmy material. When a tractor was substituted for the team the stripping efficiency on a two-row test was 96.9 percent and only 6.2 percent of stemmy material was present in the harvested flowers.

QUALITY OF MECHANICALLY HARVESTED CROP

In considering the efficiency of the harvester the quality of the material it delivers is just as important as the thoroughness with which it removes the flowers from the plants. Hand-picked flowers are naturally the basis for comparison, as these contain practically nothing but the flowers. Leaves, long stems, and foreign matter are absent when the picking is carefully done. When hand strippers or the cylinder strippers previously referred to are used a varying amount of such material is present with the flowers. With the machine herein described the ray florets are more or less torn by the rapping effect of the stripping irons on the rapidly revolving stripper rolls. This has no effect on the quality of the material but gives it a somewhat tattered appearance, which is added to by the small fragments of leaves that cling to the flowers. Short stems, either loose or attached to flowers, are also present in small amounts, but most important is the bulky, stemmy material consisting of flowers with long stems attached, some of the latter having pulled out of the crown of the plant and having usually some leaves attached to them. This is readily removed before or after drying, with a rake or fork, and a mechanical device for accomplishing this could be constructed. Short stems with flowers attached are less easily removed, but the percentage of the dry weight represented by such stems is so small that their presence affects the insecticidal value of the material only slightly. The leaves and leaf fragments and corollas of the ray florets that are present cannot be separated immediately after harvesting but can be largely removed by means of a fanning mill when the material is thoroughly dry.

To determine the proportion of these several parts present in the dried material, several pounds obtained in each of three typical field tests of the harvester at Glenn Dale, Md., in 1938 were separated into the several parts referred to and the data assembled in table 4.

It will be noted that the stemmy material, which is easily removed, and leaves comprise the principal plant parts present in the material delivered by the machine other than the loose flowers. The former is not without value, however, because when dry it consists of at least one-third flowers, and even the remainder, which is mostly stems, is not entirely worthless because the stems are usually considered to have about one-tenth the insecticidal value of the flowers. The stemmy material, removable either at the time of harvest or when dry, should, therefore, be commercially useful. There appears to be no practical way of removing the flowers from it so that the stems may be discarded. The parts removed with the fanning mill are of no value and their presence, especially that of the leaves, detracts from the appearance of the crop. However, the total amount present is usually so small that the insecticidal value of the crop is reduced only very slightly if they are not removed.

The extent to which the removal of the other plant parts mixed with the flowers as harvested affect the content of total pyrethrins is shown in table 5, in which the data obtained in the three field tests at Glenn Dale, Md., 1938, are assembled for that purpose. It may be concluded from these data that the separation of most of the leaves, corollas of ray florets, and trash with a fanning mill and the retention of the stemmy material is the most desirable procedure if the crop is to be utilized for making agricultural dusts, spray extracts, etc.

TABLE 4.—*Proportion of the various plant parts present in samples of machine-harvested air-dried material as determined by separation with fanning mill and by hand*

Test run No. [1]	Material delivered by machine				Flowers, cleaned with fanning mill	
	Total	Stemmy material [2]		Flowers, leaf fragments, corollas of ray florets, and stem pieces [3]	Leaves, corollas of ray florets [4]	Flowers with traces of leaves and stem pieces
		Flowers	Stems			
	Grams	*Grams*	*Grams*	*Grams*	*Grams*	*Grams*
1	2,366.4	43.6	79.0	2,243.8	182.0	2,061.8
2	2,864.5	94.8	226.8	2,542.9	146.3	2,396.6
3	3,242.1	146.6	337.7	2,757.8	303.7	2,454.1

Test run No. [1]	Mill-cleaned flowers further cleaned by hand [5]					Clean flowers present in machine-delivered materials[6]	Proportion of various parts in machine-delivered material		
	Small stem particles	Leaf fragments	Flowers with short stems		Clean flowers		Leaves, corollas of ray florets (no value)	Stems (some value)	Flowers (full value)
			Stems	Flowers					
	Grams	*Grams*	*Grams*	*Grams*	*Grams*	*Percent*	*Percent*	*Percent*	*Percent*
1	3.5	4.1	1.4	8.0	2,044.8	86.4	7.86	3.55	88.59
2	7.8	2.3	4.3	13.5	2,368.7	82.7	5.19	8.34	86.47
3	15.7	5.2	9.6	28.7	2,394.9	73.9	9.53	11.19	79.28

[1] Refers to test runs at Glenn Dale, Md., 1938. (See table 2.)
[2] This material is readily removed before or after drying with a fork or mechanical devices.
[3] The proportion of extraneous matter present in these flowers is very small. It cannot be removed before drying. (See footnote 4.)
[4] The fanning mill easily removes this material, which consists mostly of leaves.
[5] The separation here indicated can be accomplished only by hand, but, as shown, the leaf and stem parts are present in such small amounts that their separation is not necessary.
[6] This column shows the total percentage of flowers without stems attached in the material delivered by machine.

TABLE 5.—*Quality of the machine-harvested, air-dried material as such and after the removal of some parts by various procedures, as determined by the percentage of total pyrethrins present* [1]

Procedure	Parts removed	Percentage of total pyrethrins present		
		Test No. 1 [2]	Test No. 2 [2]	Test No. 3 [2]
None	None	0.889	0.873	0.804
Forked or raked	Stemmy material	.915	.937	.879
Cleaned only with fanning mill	Most of the leaves; corollas of ray florets, trash.	.963	.920	.887
Forked or raked and then cleaned with fanning mill.	Stemmy material; leaves, corollas of ray florets, trash.	.996	.995	.989
Forked or raked, cleaned with fanning mill, and then cleaned by hand.	Stemmy material, leaves, corollas of ray florets, small pieces of stems, and flowers with short stems.	1.000	1.000	1.000

[1] The percentage calculations in this table are made from the data given in table 4, assuming clean flowers to contain 1 percent of total pyrethrins, stems 0.1 percent, and all other parts no pyrethrins.
[2] These tests refer to the 3 field tests at Glenn Dale, Md., 1938 (table 2).

Under the present ruling of the Food and Drug Administration, pyrethrum containing less than 5 percent of stems and 2 percent of acid-insoluble ash, none of which has been intentionally added, may be labeled and sold as "insect powder" without any declaration of active and inert ingredients on the label. According to the data in table 4 the crop harvested in test No. 1, so far as concerns stem content, may be marketed as insect powder without further declarations and without the removal of any portions thereof. When the stemmy material is removed and the flowers then cleaned with a fanning mill only a very small percentage of stems remain (table 4).

Pyrethrum extracts are used in large quantities as household sprays and when so used the extracts often come in contact with furnishings, such as curtains, table linen, and clothing. It is necessary, therefore, that the extracts do not stain or otherwise injure such articles. The normal color present in extracts of pyrethrum flowers with petroleum solvents bleaches rapidly, and the sprays now mostly used will leave no stain whatever on delicate fabrics.

The question may well be raised whether some of the machine-harvested flowers, including the stems, leaves, and other material in the proportions shown in the several tables, will yield extracts that can safely be so used. To determine this by actual trial, extracts were made of the following four materials (air-dried) from each of the field tests Nos. 1 and 3 (table 2), using a petroleum solvent widely used commercially for making such extracts: (1) Material as delivered by the machine; (2) flowers after forking out the stemmy material; (3) flowers after forking out the stemmy material and removing leaves, small stems with and without flowers, corollas of ray florets, trash, etc., with a fanning mill; (4) flowers completely cleaned by fork, mill, and finally by hand (see table 4). These extracts were placed on a sheet of white paper in sufficient quantities in each case to spread over an area about 2 inches in diameter and the paper placed in a window on a partly cloudy day. All the extracts had a pronounced yellow to yellowish-green color but all evaporated and bleached completely and promptly, and no stains were left in any case. In a second test the paper was placed in diffused light in the room rather than in the window with the same results. Similar tests on cotton, rayon, and silk fabrics gave like results. From these observations it appears that the leaves and stems present in the material delivered by the machine do not interfere with its use in the manufacture of sprays for all purposes.

Although the insecticidal value of machine-harvested pyrethrum with none of the stems and leaves removed is not greatly less than that of clean, hand-picked flowers, especially when the machine is used under reasonably favorable conditions, and although the extracts of such pyrethrum leave no stain on fabrics when used as a household spray, it is nevertheless desirable that there be a practical way of separating these parts from the flowers. The stemmy material may be removed from the fresh or dry flowers with a fork or rake, or by means of a shaking device when large quantities must be handled. Most of the leaves, corollas of ray florets, and some trash are easily separated from the dried material with a fanning mill, there remaining with the flowers after that only small proportions of leaf and stem particles, the retention of which does not seriously affect the insecticidal value and marketability of the crop.

SUMMARY AND CONCLUSIONS

Pyrethrum, an important insecticide, consisting of the dried flowers of several species of *Chrysanthemum*, mainly *C. cinerariaefolium*, is produced in Japan, Yugoslavia, Brazil, and Kenya, Africa, where the plant is grown under cultivation. It is adapted to many sections of the United States, and experiments have shown that flowers of acceptable potency can be grown here. However, its introduction as a crop in this country has been prevented by the lack of a practical and economical method of harvesting the flowers. The characteristics of the plant and flower and their relation to the requirements of a practical harvester are discussed, and the several methods of harvesting by a number of devices that have heretofore been used or proposed, none of which have been satisfactory, are reviewed.

With a modified cotton stripper results were obtained that suggested the general principles of a successful harvester. After numerous trials under a variety of crop conditions a machine was built in which a pair of stripping rollers were mounted as a unit on a corn-binder frame, thus making use of the binder-bull wheel, side hitch, and pick-up chains.

The salient features of the machine are diagrammatically illustrated and data showing the efficiency of its performance under various conditions and with various adjustments are assembled in convenient tables. On fairly level ground and with straight rows and if the plants are not badly lodged the machine will deliver about 95 percent of the crop. The efficiency is also determined by the degree of maturity of the flowers. At the preferred stage for harvesting they are stripped from the stems easily, but as they begin to ripen the stems become tough. Weather conditions also affect the ease with which the flowers may be removed, and if, due to unfavorable seasonal conditions, the flower stems are shorter than 15 inches many of them will pass under the machine without passing through the stripping rollers. If the soil is too rich or of a nature that causes rank growth the flower stems will tangle and lodge, which also reduces the efficiency of the machine.

It is estimated that with this machine two persons can harvest the flowers from at least 4 acres of pyrethrum in a day, as compared with seven persons required to harvest 1 acre a day by a semi-mechanized method used in Pennsylvania where it was found to be tedious and expensive.

The quality of the crop when harvested with such a machine is discussed with respect to its general usefulness for various commercial products, and practical methods are described of removing from the harvested flowers the moderate quantity of stems and leaves that are present. Extracts were made of the flowers containing the leaves and stems in the proportion in which they occur in harvested material, using a commercial solvent, and it was demonstrated by satisfactory tests that such extracts when used as sprays will not stain various fabrics.

ORGANIZATION OF THE UNITED STATES DEPARTMENT OF AGRICULTURE WHEN THIS PUBLICATION WAS LAST PRINTED

Secretary of Agriculture	CLAUDE R. WICKARD.
Under Secretary	PAUL H. APPLEBY.
Assistant Secretary	GROVER B. HILL.
Director of Information	MORSE SALISBURY.
Director of Extension Work	M. L. WILSON.
Director of Finance	W. A. JUMP.
Director of Personnel	ROY F. HENDRICKSON.
Director of Research	JAMES T. JARDINE.
Director of Marketing	MILO R. PERKINS.
Solicitor	MASTIN G. WHITE.
Land Use Coordinator	M. S. EISENHOWER.
Office of Plant and Operations	ARTHUR B. THATCHER, Chief.
Office of C. C. C. Activities	FRED W. MORRELL, Chief.
Office of Experiment Stations	JAMES T. JARDINE, Chief.
Office of Foreign Agricultural Relations	LESLIE A. WHEELER, Director.
Agricultural Adjustment Administration	R. M. EVANS, Administrator.
Bureau of Agricultural Chemistry and Engineering.	HENRY G. KNIGHT, Chief.
Bureau of Agricultural Economics	H. R. TOLLEY, Chief.
Agricultural Marketing Service	C. W. KITCHEN, Chief.
Bureau of Animal Industry	JOHN R. MOHLER, Chief.
Commodity Credit Corporation	CARL B. ROBBINS, President.
Commodity Exchange Administration	JOSEPH M. MEHL, Chief.
Bureau of Dairy Industry	O. E. REED, Chief.
Bureau of Entomology and Plant Quarantine	LEE A. STRONG, Chief.
Farm Credit Administration	A. G. BLACK, Governor.
Farm Security Administration	C. B. BALDWIN, Administrator.
Federal Crop Insurance Corporation	LEROY K. SMITH, Manager.
Forest Service	EARLE H. CLAPP, Acting Chief.
Bureau of Home Economics	LOUISE STANLEY, Chief.
Library	RALPH R. SHAW, Librarian.
Bureau of Plant Industry	E. C. AUCHTER, Chief.
Rural Electrification Administration	HARRY SLATTERY, Administrator.
Soil Conservation Service	H. H. BENNETT, Chief.
Surplus Marketing Administration	MILO R. PERKINS, Administrator.

This circular is a joint contribution from

Bureau of Plant Industry	E. C. AUCHTER, Chief.
Division of Drug and Related Plants	W. W. STOCKBERGER, Principal Physiologist, in Charge.
Bureau of Agricultural Chemistry and Engineering.	HENRY G. KNIGHT, Chief.
Division of Farm Mechanical Equipment Research.	R. B. GRAY, Principal Agricultural Engineer, in Charge.

U S GOVERNMENT PRINTING OFFICE. 1941

Lightning Source UK Ltd.
Milton Keynes UK
UKHW050428071118
331792UK00005BB/200/P